Another Way Home

Beau Beausoleil

BLUE LIGHT PRESS
1st WORLD
PUBLISHING

San Francisco | Fairfield | Delhi

Another Way Home

Beau Beausoleil

Copyright ©2022 by Beau Beausoleil

First Edition.

ISBN: 978-1-4218-3716-1

Library of Congress Cataloging-in-Publication Data

1ST WORLD LIBRARY
PO Box 2211
Fairfield, Iowa 52556
www.1stworldpublishing.com

BLUE LIGHT PRESS
www.bluelightpress.com
Email: bluelightpress@aol.com

Cover Art and design by Andrea Hassiba

For Andrea, my muse in all ways.

Acknowledgements

Some of these poems first appeared in: The news of the day…., The Weird Times, Hello Goodbye Apocalypse, The Blake-Jones Review, and Pandemic Puzzle Poems.

An Introduction to Beau Beausoleil's New Writing

I love the way Beau Beausoleil's poems catch hold of the invisible. They always travel to a mysterious place that transcends the appearances of the world. He reveals what cannot be expressed with ordinary language – sometimes the grief of life, sometimes the joy, sometimes what you can only see in a dream. His work embodies the inventiveness of the Language Poets but goes further, leading us through the images with a compelling narrative voice and a luminous spiritual vision. *Another Way Home* contains his best new writing.

In this book, you will find an exploration of what matters – love, life, death, passion, memory, dream, what is invisible.

"They follow each root
down past
the sleeping page
to the crumbling
stars above them"

His poems give profound attention to the interior world, but always informed by images of the world around him, making his work both visionary and grounded.

"They listen intently
to the traffic
of their interior
language
before they
cross the street
to work"

Beausoleil writes poems that invite you to see the world differently
– to see more, feel more, and pay attention to those moments where
life leaps off the page, often quietly.

"Poetry begins
when the
camera
leaves the
two main
characters
and tracks
instead
the geography
of everything
on the table
between them"

He often steps into the role of poet as the conscience of the society.

"The radio
in my
rusting bones
keeps saying
the name
of my country
as if it were
a storm
approaching"

In these poems, he also celebrates a loving marriage which keeps
blooming over time.

"Your tongue
on her skin
filling with
the salt taste
of the
far away
sea"

When I was a graduate student at San Francisco State University,
Beau Beausoleil was already a celebrated poet, held in high regard
among my fellow students and faculty. He was already one of San
Francisco's best. Through time, his vision and his writing continue
to get deeper and deeper – life does this to poets who pay attention
to the world and what is inside them.

Another Way Home
is a book to read
slowly
carefully
with delight
and appreciation.

– Diane Frank, Chief Editor, Blue Light Press
Author of *While Listening to the Enigma Variations: New and Selected
Poems*

HERE

(for Javier)

I wave
to my
grandson
as he
pretends
to fly
around
the backyard

Then his
small arms
catch hold
of the
invisible
and as
he lifts
off the
ground

he pulls
me up
too

ON THE SECOND DAY

My body keeps
trying to fall
and take root
in words

I raise my hands
above my head
calling to
the storms
of mercy to
come this way

I want to
sink below
the quiet
muted song

I want to
let go of
beauty
And roughly
hold closer
to the days
that keep
leaving me
behind

The Sunflowers

1.
There is less light
coming through
the cloth clouds
than before

but I see things now
in a fist of clarity

When they punch
the needle in

a place of blood
rises up

2.
I ran up the stairs
to pray for the dead

I ran back down
to begin my own dying

3.
I want to
walk with you
through the fields
of wordless light

I want us to be together

as each day is plowed
back underneath the night

AT THIS DISTANCE

I am sleeping
in your dream
as I write this

We are
so near
the violet
mountains
that they
breathe for us

And
once more
the gentle
reed boat
carries us
away from
those
we never
really
loved enough

A Field

The moon has
positioned itself
just out of
reach

Closer
is the serpent tongue
restless on the branch
above me

I briefly saw
a way back
to something
that never
existed

the sky
around us
remains
uncertain
in its
direction

Once more
I lie down
under this
ruined field
and allow the
rooted earth
to harvest
me

I Want To Tell You

There is
nothing
personal
in our
breathing

Where there
is suffering
we turn
the bodies
over

We live
as stones
in the
shallows

with the
weight of
our words
holding us
down

Dog
Observations
(for Bella)

Dogs
forgive
the sins
we have
yet to
commit

they bark
out of
car
windows
like signal
flags

they respect
our choices of
personal attire
and life
partners
and find
every direction
that we throw
the ball
both perfect
and intriguing

They secretly
hope
that years
after
they die
we will
dig up
one of
their bones
and carry
it around
in our mouth
until dinner

BEFORE SLEEP

And in these
days of
painful witness
we call on the
hard earned
stupid grace
of our lives
to hold us
together

OUR SIMPLE KNOWLEDGE

The longing of birds
overwhelms me

and how they live
in their kingdoms

without walls or
windows

and finally die
where they fall
from a single branch
of their sky

without ever acknowledging
our existence

A Dream Journey

I deliver myself
into the next step
up the stone path

I am carrying
another handful
of hollow words

My intention
is always
to set them
down
one by one
on an empty
page

Until
I fill my
uncertain
memory
with their
glancing light

OF MEMORY

All these
books

as alone
as I am
in my
poems

I'm leaving
their words
behind

I'm going
from here

as far as
the night
takes me
while I sleep

And then
I'll walk
to the
edge of
each empty
winter field

and call
out your
name

not looking back

until I see you
coming towards me

WORDS EXCHANGED
IN PASSING CARS

It is not the sturdy
wooden beams
that raise
the house
aloft
that I study

but instead
the rotting
wooden plank

still dark
and wet

that has
washed ashore
alone
that will hold
my attention
forever

CHALK LINES

I cut
one slice
of bread
and fit it
into the
toaster

I pull
the red mug
down from
the shelf

the coffee
slips into it
so easily

I stare out
the kitchen window
at the green
waving sour grass

I lift my cup
to the small
yellow flowers
and the wildness
that always
returns

I listen closely
to the intersections
of traffic between
my words

I wonder
if my powdery bones
will settle tonight
on a coastline
that I might already know

ANOTHER WAY HOME

The stars
stand off
to one side
of the inked sky
and think of us

wanting us
closer

wondering
how they
might reach
into us

and gently touch
again
the burning
ashen cold of our
lives

In Our Native Tongue

The longer
I looked
at the apples
in the marketplace

the more
I wanted to
find
the one that
was still
in the tree

and bring it
to you

What we all want
to bite into
what we each want
to taste again

is what
has slipped
from our grasp

and fallen back

among the leaves
and limbs
that try to drown us
each waking night

THE TRANSIT OF HOURS

1.

The dream
never lifts
until it
harms me

and for a time
nothing moves

except
my escaping breath

2.

The day
would form
without me

but it waits

and often
I pity its generosity

On The Curve

1.

The empty city streets
are gradually losing
their intent and purpose

they seem like
ancient worn monuments
with just a whisper of human
habitation

2.

The front of each house
is filled with praise
while the back of each house
is filled with fear

3.

In fairness to the clouds
we sleep
under another landscape

we cover our bodies
and fall
without asking the sky
to remember anything about us

EVERYTHING
SUBTRACTED

A bird moves
the sky back
for a moment

I see the black coast
of infinity pass
to the side of
my eye

We are
not needed
in the desire of planets
and stars

but we live
wanting that

See
how that bird
climbs into the sky

See how

the day
is bent along
those lines of
our watching

Birds
part dream / part
tongue of regret

Trees full
of birds
falling
upwards

each song persisting
as we hear it
fly away

THE LOOSENING

There is so much
open water
at the borders
of this page

oceans deepened
by love and cruelty

I know the
missing shorelines
by habit
and I try to find them
in my fitful sleep

I think about
my life as a repeated
testimony of drowning

And I know that
I've stayed at one end of it
held in the undertow
of every specific sorrow

I examine the waves
and how they break
against the same obstacles
again and again

I am always hoping to loosen
each breath from my body

I keep waiting for things
in my past to change

RED WAGON

I didn't want to
make the long
journey to
my birth

I wanted to keep
to the path of
the almost
night

I wanted
the falling wind
to turn me
away from here
forever

but I heard you
dreaming
each night

a song so tender
and harsh with beauty
that it made me
want to sing with you

and so I came here

VOYAGE

He found her note
years later
between the pages
of a book called
Arctic Sea Ice

The note
on tissue thin
blue writing
paper
said that
the Titanic
left a stain
on the iceberg
that sank it

I am
sinking
too
she wrote

have I left any stain
on you

FORGOTTEN DIRECTIONS

Some days
I have a
small part
in my own
waking life

And it's then
that I meet you
at the kitchen table
where we argue
with the newspaper
in great satisfaction

And then together
we set out through
the day in our usual
blessed madness

Other days
we sit across
from each other
but have no
lines to speak

We go from there
into the world
in silence
like the small
fledgling that
found shelter
near our
front door
and later
disappeared

In the last
of the evening
I sit alone
to write this poem
as a way of saying
your name

Waiting For You

I look
at each line
in the poem
wondering
which sequence
of words
will betray me

Which line
will take
my reader
to a door
that I don't
want to open

My poems
are like
the narrow
hallways
in cheap
hotels

With or
without
a key
With or
without a
companion
There is never
any room
to turn around

A Secondhand Alphabet

History
has been
wretched
today
unbalanced
in the favor
of suffering

I keep seeing
beauty as it is
almost lost
As in
the fold
of water
over my
hands
as I
wash
them

The
plums
so full of
taste
are falling
to the
ground

we pause
in time
to gather
them

All these
infinite
small parts
of the day
keep getting
in the way
of my dying

ALONG THE WAY

I needed
an anchor
to wrap
my arms
around
on the way
to work
or I just
wouldn't
get there

I needed a map of
crossed out
destinations
to watch out for
in case my rusted
ink car
started
up again
and ran over
another page

How many hot
asphalt hours
of listening
to wrecked
versions of my
unmade life
did I need
to hear
from a
fading radio
in my head

How many exits
after this one
was it
before I could
open my eyes

ANOTHER CROSSING

Some
days
don't come
straight
at you
instead they
arrive
by way
of a
stranger
who has
returned
from
a long
journey
and now
sits close
with her
eyes
closed
remembering
aloud
the names
of those
who died
on certain
days
along the way

THE WAY
THE MORNING
STARTS

A Crow
takes your
new poem
in her beak
and flies
over the
houses
to the
edge of
the river
where poems
are traded
for bread

When she flies
back
you have made
coffee
and as you
cut the bread
with honey
you sing
a praise song
for her wisdom
and beauty
and for
the small poems

that still grow
in the
stone fields
of your life

THREE
FRAGMENTS
OF A
PARABLE

1.
You
left
a note
written
on moving
water

2.
You
altered
a Caravaggio
to depict
a worker
being nailed to
a factory floor

3.
Two trucks
appear on
the coast road
carrying
yellow onions

they pass us
with their
green tarps
flapping
in the wind

Lives Of
The Poets

On
the bus
to work
you
see a
mother
bend
to tie
the shoe
of her
young
daughter
and in
that
ordinary
moment
you
feel
a kind of
quiet
grace
that
pulls
the
light
closer
and
brings
for a

few
seconds
a stillness
to everyone
nearby

How Grief
Is Assembled

The
dead
repeat
their names
to those
passing by
who see
only small
birds holding
onto the wind

Tell my
loved ones
they plead
where they
can find
my bones
and glasses

Some days
you are
afraid to
read the
words
in any book
you pick up

Even
clouds and
stars fall
into the
dark earth
without
warning

You stand
in the kitchen
watching
the kettle boil
listening
to its
violent steam

OUT OF
THIS

Sleep
discards you
and goes on
to another

The pale
morning
light
of
someone
still dreaming
holds you

shows you
the way
to the
kitchen

You stand
at the
sink
counting
how many
mountains
are still
standing

You examine
the color
of the
coffee
in your
cup

imagining
a black sea
inside
your unnamed life

LINES

Some days arrive
because there is
nowhere else
to go

I awake
without
thinking
on the way
to work

I write
down
the words
that brought
me here

I hide
the poems
in my
open hands

To Be Here

The imprecise
movement
of a dream
falling from
sleep and
landing in
a stand
of trees
is unknown
to me

To have
trouble
and no
voice
speaking
that anyone
can hear
is to have
no sense
of how
to find
sleep
by itself
waiting
for you

And our bodies
in turn
feel compelled
to leave us

LISTEN

The solace
you seek
is to be
found
in curling
your body
to hers

the quiet
around her
shames you

Your tongue
on her skin
filling with
the salt taste
of the
far away
sea

there is no
further reach
of meaning

COMING
HOME

At the door
we catch
our falling
bodies
in time

Behind
our
backs
two
fields
soak
up
a
steady
rain

Where
else
in this
same
world
are
there
roads
moving
away
from us
at the
speed

of light

IN CROW COUNTRY

They
held
relics
in their
beaks
of who
you had
been
before
your father
was born

And
under the
shadow
of a falling
tree your
first mother
flew away
without
you ever
waking

FAR AWAY

I cross the street
to my childhood
and find myself
waiting for the
changing light
as I walk
to the store
for my mother

I cross back over
and write down
these words
out of order
and find myself
closer to where
I want to be

far away

On The Third Day Of Drowning

The uneven
sea drops us
down
below sleep

The light in
our left eye
turns from
arctic blue
to rust
green

the
distorted sun
is lodged
somewhere
laboring
above us

What is
evident
is that
the sea
enjoys
our stroking
arms

even as we
sink from sight

AT RISK

I watch myself
move down
a line of
parked cars
trying to open
each door

my words
come apart
in the air
and fall to
the ground
while around
me each
discarded leaf
tries to
fall up
and regain
its branch

the day
leans
far back
into the
almost night

And
I ask once more
who will forgive
our hearts
in their small
indiscretions

Up
The
Street

Maybe someone
would like to
take away a
bag of my
muddy bones
and lean them
up against
some kitchen
chairs
as holy relics

maybe there's
more
to this than I
understand

I have to go back
and talk to all
the saints
on the
sidewalk

I have
to go home and
watch myself
sleep / in case
I never wake up

EARLY VALENTINE

(for A.H.)

I was
trying to
leave
one night
when you
dragged me
to the edge
of a field
and knelt
to move aside
the knotted
rooted earth
below my
body

I fell away
from my
shadow

and loved
you

LOST HARBORS

We live
on one coast
of a country
stunned by
hate and
beauty

this rusted
rising sun
as a returning
companion

we live
in a city
of language
and speak
with tongues
that sometimes
love us

there is a
multitude
of dying
in and
around us

If we were
farmers and
if this were
a film
and not
a country
we might
consider

RITUAL NEIGHBORHOOD

Black
paved
street
matching
the black
sky filled
with
metered
stars

Winter
rain
hitting
the bus
shelter
we mourn
the buried
fields of
discarded
mountains

We kiss
in the
heat of
returning
our library
books
How can
we go

home
when our
love is so
rooted in
the senses
of this
city

TRYING
TO
WRITE

Sometimes
I carry
one word
in my
mouth
all day
the way
a cat
carries a
dead
mouse
from
room to
room

looking for
someone

Sometimes
I experience
a failure
of language
and have
to call out
in silence

And
sometimes
I look
at myself
but only
write down
what the
words
let me
see

A
Relentless
Morning

There are
mornings
when my
words
can't agree
on anything

And when
I sit
opposite
to you
at the
kitchen
table
the world
rushes into
my eyes
and darkens

Some days
one needs
an art
of cellular
shock
to awaken
you say
Some days

one needs
to drain
the color
out of every
momentary
sky
to just begin

How Poets Measure Days

Poets
believe in
everything
below their
knees

crawling
infants
and
black
beetles
red
chalk clouds
and
sleeping dogs
all capture their
infinite attention

Poets
believe
in what
they
cannot
remember

They
find joy
some days
in scraping
each page
with their
muddy shoes

I Write You From Another Room

Tell my
mother
that I
taste her voice
sometimes
in my coffee

tell my
father to
drive
along the
old border
between us

tell my
sister
that there
is a swing
here that
reaches
another sky

tell my
brother
that we will
walk together
to the next
winter solstice

and you
my only
love

I want
to see
you
before I
never live
again

THIRTY-SIX
VIEWS
OF AN
EMPTY
PAGE

Yesterday
the words
were an
unbearable
fever
seeking
only to
break me
down
with no
sympathy

Today
I am
nearly
singing
when
they
lift the
weight
of living
from my
body
for just
a few
seconds

A
STONE
SKY

I have
a falling
shadow
visible
only to
someone
weeping
nearby

I fill
my oldest
wounds
with salt
and honey
and wait
through
a lifetime
for them
to heal

HERE THE MOTHER

The
smaller
clouds
shade her
weariness
as she
drives
along the
edge
of this
May
morning

One
hand
on the
turning
wheel
she
reaches
over
to caress
your face

A Moment
Of Belief

I have
brought four
green
blue pears
from the
oldest tree
and placed
them in the
yellow bowl
on the
kitchen
table

I sit
alone
waiting
for you
as the
morning
light
touches
each pear
in turn

On
The
Clock

Every word
hides another
word
lost to me

Every line
of words
has a holy
immeasurable
weight

I can
see that
knowledge
in the face
of some
strangers
on the
bus or
in line
at the
super
market

their
scarred
shifting
musical
bodies
betray their
absence from
some
loosely
held
Heaven

I did not
choose
to be among
the liars
the fallen
and the poets

I simply
showed up
for work

A BONE SONG

Some hours
I find myself
still asleep
in the
deepest
part of
the forest

the years
going by
like clouds

Some nights
I am
a single
pebble
in the
river
of trees
above me

the water
passing over
me
so cold
and sweet

Sometimes
I call out
to my
night
fever
to live
for me
so that
I might
finish my
dream
of you

FINDING THE BORDERS

1.

The hurt
in your heart
traveled down
to your shoes

Think again
they said

Think again
but not of us

2.

Some stranger
in the street
holds the light
inside us

follows us

until
we are tossed
into the cold of heaven

3.

The numbers of days
break up in our hands

as we carry God
back down the stairs

in translation

4..

The planets
keep to their borders

But the burning small stars

even as we extinguish
all the hope in them

continue to fall to the ground
between us

Plus One

I hear
Chet Baker

playing softly
as if
on a faraway
radio

His notes an echo
of a whisper

The rasp
of his trumpet

turning into
the ache of
a song

And I listen for
a long time

at the kitchen table

looking down
at my hands

at the hesitant lines
that I write
in my open notebook

And then I start
to play something
with my words

Until I gather myself
and try to step into
his harmony

ONE MOMENT

The day
comes
to rest
in
the
black
curving
lines
that
you
draw
above
my words
I awaken
to see you
your arms
a little
akimbo
your kiss
is one more way
of knowing

Valentine

Love is
sometimes
simple

See how
the tree
embraces
the light

Love
can be
noisy
or quietly
sleeping
for days

The moon
sometimes
becomes shy
and throws a
shadow
over us

to give us some quiet
some room to be alone

ONE DAY
BEFORE VALENTINE'S
DAY

They kiss
deeply

And
together
loosen
their grip
on the
Earth

Some say
that is too
intimate
a moment
to put
in a
poem

But
poetry
like
love

does
not
always
observe
the rules

that hold us
to gravity

DEPARTURE

There is
nothing that
scrapes away
hope
like the call
for documents

And this is often
followed
by

a disturbance
in the stars
you wished upon

POEM FOR THE NEW YEAR

The self-
destructive sun
has held
me in her
embrace
for another
year

her sweat
glistens
on my
winter body

I dream of her
in the traffic
of stars

I dream
of making
my way
with her
toward
the old
station

And when
the train
arrives
and then
departs
without us
I see the
two of us
following
the torn up
tracks for
another year
all the way
home

My Childhood

I am still lost
in my mind
most days

But I know
with some
certainty

that
if I am here
I am not
back there
with you

unless imagined

I try
to tear
each
thought
apart
and sit
down beside
the lightless
window

I listen to
my heart
punch my
body

There are
some knots of
memory
that always
remain visible
but absent
to me

always
just out of reach
of any words

THE
ADORATION

The next
Messenger
will be
She who
is born
on this day
near an apartment
house
after someone
closes their eyes
below the awning
of a corner
grocery store
on a summer
sidewalk
thousands
of miles away

The flat
city surfaces
of our
kitchen tables
accommodate
the fields
of hallways
and the
children who
all cry in the
same language

The Angels
line up
their shoes
at the door

They have come
a great distance
to hear
the newborn
sing

POET

There are days
when a poem
cannot protect you
when beauty
overtakes you
in the smallest
detail of light
shifting from
leaf to leaf

There are days
when you have to
turn away from
the dreaming wind

Days when you
can only swim
to the night shore
without direction
or understanding

ABSOLVED
OF
MEANING

My soul
has worn out
its ragged
clothes
but clings
to my bones
alongside
the buried
riverbank
waiting for
the reed boat
to carry me
across my
dying
towards
another shore
of morning

BLUE COLOR
BLUE COLOR

Holding
light

I see it
in some
words

Always
with
the need
to remember

SEA LEVEL

The
cherry
red dog
of war
rests his
head
in my lap

The
blood
on my
knuckles has
softened into
stone

The oldest
tongue
in my
body
wants me
to run
from the
burning
trees

WITHOUT OUR CONSCIOUSNESS

The insect
slowly
crossing
the green
leaf
pauses to
absorb its
own
perception
of beauty

SLOW LIGHT

Trying
to hold
onto
the last
color
of our
waking
when
the slow
light
comes
to find
us

We have
no map
only the
steady
direction
of falling

Outside
our voices
the rusted
hinge
of the
sidewalk
marks our
leaving

How We Cross Over

We
exchange
vows
with the
passing
cars
and cross
the streets
holding up
traffic
in signs
following
the radiant
darkness
that surrounds
our uneven
entry into
any night

AUGUST 16TH

(for Andrea)

I get
up early
to watch
the light
carefully
undo the
knotted dark

It's your
birthday
so
I pull
a white
rabbit
out of
a poem

We kiss
then cut
the cake
and hope
the burning
California
sky
is not
a candle
for anyone's
coming year

ON LISBON STREET

I ask only that
the patron saint
of birthday wishes
help me salvage
the bones of my
sunken childhood

I ask only that
the patron saint
of empty chairs
show me how
to forget that
I am breathing

I ask only that
the patron saint
of misaligned directions
show me
another quadrant
on the map
of my own
collapsing universe

And when the
patron saint of
backyard moons
lies down to sleep
behind my closing eyes

I ask only to lie down
with her

ON MY WAY
TO THE KITCHEN

I elbow
past
the fallen
angels
smoking
in the
hallway

I walk
under
the clouds
looking for
lightning

I step
over the
undelivered
love letters
past the
imperfect
lies and
unmeasured
tears

Arriving
at last
at my
first cup
of coffee
I sit
motionless
looking down into
the dark water
of safe passage
trying to catch
another glimpse
of my fading
lucky star

THINK
AGAIN

Small
scattering
birds
realign
the sky after
storms and
keep the
ragged edges
of dying stars
smooth to the
touch

I don't really
want to
go anywhere
that doesn't
have a moon
or two

The guy
at the
post office
said that
my letter
to myself
might
never get
to me
despite

the best
of his
intentions

MUSEUM DAYS

I saw
one of
Sylvia
Plath's
typewriters
behind
glass
with a
typed
poem
stuck
in the
roller

they were
her own
two spirit
animals
pacing
back and
forth in
complete
raging
stillness

watching
me as I
stared at
them

I wish now
that I had
smashed
the glass
and set
them free

THE
NARROW
SKY

I sing all
night
to the
migrating
birds above
me

asking that
they carry
a message
to my
loved ones

that
I am
moving slowly
through this
crooked
narrow sky
with only
my one good
wing to lean
on

say
I will
one day
join them

that no matter
what else
happens

I still know
the way

My
Favorite
Poets

1.
They let
the words
wrap
themselves
around and
around them
until they share
the same breath

2.
They follow each root
down past
the sleeping page
to the crumbling
stars above them

3.
They listen intently
to the traffic
of their interior
language
before they
cross the street
to work

A
Resemblance
To Memory

I used to
like it
when we
talked out
of words

I liked it
when we
would
lie down
together
to wait for
the rain to
start hitting
the windows

We used to
know our
way around
hallways and
coastlines

now our
attention
is focused
on words

I never noticed
the night until
it began to arrive
so much earlier
on its own

Out In The World

The radio
in my
rusting bones
keeps saying
the name
of my country
as if it were
a storm
approaching

I have to
get up
and turn
myself
around to
lie back
down on
the map of
my country's
treachery and
disappointment

We only
have to
watch the
lifeless moon
move along
the border
to understand
how cold
and distant
we can be
to anyone

POEM FOR
MY COUNTRY

I want
a day
when
every
gun
refuses
to
fire

I want
a day
when
every
hateful
word
stings
the tongue
of its
speaker

I want
a day
of listening
only to the
under/sky
of dreaming
earth
I want
a first day

to hold
our country
to its
promises

I want
a day
that does
not end
in grief

SHOPTALK

Poetry begins
when the
camera
leaves the
two main
characters
and tracks
instead
the geography
of everything
on the table
between them

CALIFORNIA FIRES

The sun
is late
this
orange
pigment
ashen
dark
September
morning
having
feverishly
first
risen
thousands
of miles
away
in
the black
coffee
sky
above
a
roadside
diner
parking
lot

THE WIND
OFF THE
OCEAN

I hear
the small
bells along
the river
as I float
down the
palm of my
hand

there is
no distance
before me
only time
unfolding
behind me

In The Folded Night

She carried you
in her arms
outside
to watch
the moon
dance below
every rising
star

This was
the second way
your mother
brought you
into
this world

EARLY
MORNING

If you escape
I will look
for the
two horses
that brought
us here

If you
double back
for me
I will
shake the
earth
that covers
my dying

I want
to sing
again
on the
roan horse
and watch
all of history
pass us by